Thinking skills
PSHE & Citizenship Activities

Pat Hollingbery

Section 1

- **Developing confidence and responsibility and making the most of their abilities**

Section 2

- **Preparing to play an active role as citizens**

Section 3

- **Developing a healthy, safer lifestyle**

Section 4

- **Developing good relationships and respecting the differences between people**

Published by Hopscotch Educational Publishing Ltd,
Unit 2, The Old Brushworks, 56 Pickwick Road, Corsham,
Wiltshire, SN13 9BX (Tel: 01249 701701)

© 2002 Hopscotch Educational Publishing
Reprinted 2003

Written by Pat Hollingbery
Series design by Blade Communications
Illustrated by Bernard Connors
Cover illustrated by Pat Murray
Reprinted by Ashford Colour Press Ltd

Pat Hollingbery hereby asserts her moral right to be
identified as the author of this work in accordance
with the Copyright, Designs and Patents Act, 1988.

ISBN 1-902239-93-8

Developing responsible citizens

Today's teacher is being encouraged to take a more holistic approach to teaching and learning. The aim is to develop children who are well-rounded individuals, thoughtful, sensitive, critical thinkers with transferable skills which will serve them better in life than mere facts ever could.

To help teachers fulfil this wider role of developing responsible citizens, the subject areas of 'PSHE and Citizenship' and 'Thinking Skills' were added to the National Curriculum. These provide a three-pronged attack upon a perceived modern malaise, in which the boundaries between right and wrong seem to be blurring; excessive consumerism is considered admirable; and ethical values appear to be in decline. Peer pressure and family influence, while often positive and life enhancing, are occasionally highly destructive and some children will only be encouraged to adopt acceptable modes of behaviour through the influence of their school.

Taking responsibility

Young people need to understand that, not only do choices exist, but they also have the power to make such choices for themselves. That their peers or family members may behave in an irresponsible manner does not automatically mean that they too must act in such a way. They have free will and should be encouraged to exercise it wisely. They must take responsibility for their own behaviour and not blame others for their own shortcomings. As well as having choice, they also have the ability to say 'No'.

Breeding success

This book offers numerous activities that address the areas of 'PSHE and Citizenship' and 'Thinking Skills'. Many are discussion-based, although a variety of approaches have been used. Some children who may be under-achieving academically will shine in activities such as these, which deal with aspects of life that are real and of importance to them, such as bullying and racism. The greater their interest in the subject-matter, the greater their level of participation is likely to be, which may well lead to an increase in self-confidence and self-esteem, as their views are listened to and respected by others.

Feeling secure

Before attempting the activities, it is important that the children are in a familiar, supportive, non-threatening environment. The activities should be modified, if necessary, to suit the age range of the children and the time available.

It is imperative to show sensitivity, particularly when grouping children. A group that works well together will enable an activity to succeed. Children should not be forced to participate in all of the exercises – particularly those that deal with sensitive issues. A balance should be struck between encouragement and insistence. Although group members must have the right not to share their thoughts and feelings, on learning that others have similar problems or opinions to their own, they may subsequently feel able to disclose things which they had previously kept hidden. Teachers should always remain vigilant for signs of abuse.

Becoming thoughtful

Everyone should be encouraged to take a positive approach to the activities, listening to others and respecting their views, while not necessarily agreeing with them. Teachers and group members must also respect confidentiality, while encouraging openness and honesty. Make sure that the children understand that they will be expected to justify their statements and views wherever possible. This will develop their thinking skills as they do so. They will also need to learn how to give and receive criticism effectively, without an attitude of malice or one-upmanship.

Flexibility is important here; changing one's mind is not to be seen as a sign of weakness, but as the result of gathering more reliable or more convincing information. Hopefully, in time, the automatic response will become a thing of the past; instead children will give considered replies to thoughtful questions. They will take the time to think things through before they speak, weighing up their own statements and those of others, looking for any hidden meanings that at first sight may not be apparent. They should be encouraged to consider matters from their own perspective, and also take into account the perspective of others.

Moulding views and opinions

Children and teachers alike should be prepared for their views to be challenged, with teachers leading by example and showing flexibility, tolerance, patience, fairness and thoughtfulness, as well as being non-judgemental. The teacher should be more of a facilitator during these activities, enabling the children to develop their own thinking skills, rather than being force-fed information and facts. In such an environment, listening and communication skills are of paramount importance. It is here that long-lasting views may be shaped.

Thinking for themselves

In schools today the development of effective thinking skills should be uppermost in teachers' minds. Without the ability to think and reason, mere facts will be of little use; hence a primary aim of this book is to encourage children to think for themselves.

Many of the activities will involve children in dialogue and it is during such dialogue that thinking skills are most likely to be developed. They will be able to learn from one another and the quality of the learning may well be demonstrably better than if they were working alone. They will be able to feed off one another's ideas when brainstorming a problem and any possible solutions are liable to be more wide-ranging and creative in a group situation. This is especially the case when open-ended questions are used and when group members are encouraged to challenge one another if their reasoning appears to be unsound.

It is unlikely that problems raised here will have incontrovertible solutions, so the teacher should not be expected to hold all the answers. In a normal, subject-related question-and-answer session, children are often asked to come up with answers that the teacher already knows. If their thinking leads them in novel directions, such answers are often considered merely to be wrong.

When dealing with issues of a more ethical nature, where straightforward answers are less apparent, the teacher will also be seeking viable solutions. The children will need to come to their own conclusions, based on a sharing of ideas and views and on the understanding that they are not necessarily searching for one definitive answer. Several solutions or, indeed, no solution at all may be available.

The children will be thinking as they listen to the views of others; they will be thinking as they formulate their own ideas; they will be thinking as they express these ideas and as they weigh up the meanings behind what they and their peers have said. They will be thinking as they chastise themselves for missing an opportunity to speak, or for speaking inappropriately. They will need to concentrate on the problem in hand and keep their thinking relevant. In short, they will need to be mentally alert.

Inclusivity, quality and added value

Inclusivity

These activities are likely to appeal to a variety of learning styles, some of which are not always adequately catered for. By offering plentiful opportunities for dialogue, those less confident with reading and writing, for example, will not be prevented from participating actively. Even the least able children will have their own views on matters such as road safety and healthy living, which they will be able to express verbally. Even the quietest, most reticent children will be able to have their say within a supportive, non-threatening environment. Children who have found themselves to be 'different' or excluded from full participation for some reason, perhaps those lacking in self-confidence due to racism or bullying, may begin to find greater acceptance as they are encouraged to express their own thoughts and feelings openly, perhaps giving their tormentors the opportunity to understand them more fully.

Quality

This refers to 'quality time', where children and teachers alike are working towards solutions. They will be treating one another with consideration and respect, listening to one another's views, tolerating and accepting differences of opinion.

Added value

That there is 'added value' could refer to any resultant spin-off, such as children gradually developing a more thoughtful attitude, which eventually spills over into their everyday life.

Building citizens

It would be wrong of us to expect, or insist, that our children take on our own set of values and beliefs, but by showing them alternatives, by giving them choices and the opportunity to make these choices for themselves, we are developing in them both the confidence and the capacity to make considered decisions. As the Institute of Citizenship believes, 'No one becomes an active citizen by accident. Like anything else it has to be learned.' Hopefully this book will go some way towards achieving this aim.

How this book works

There are four sections in this book. They are based on the four sections of the PSHE and Citizenship guidelines in the National Curriculum. They are:

- Developing confidence and responsibility and making the most of their abilities
- Preparing to play an active role as citizens
- Developing a healthy, safer lifestyle
- Developing good relationships and respecting the differences between people

From each of these sections specific objectives have been selected as the basis for a game or activity.

Objectives

Each activity has two lists of objectives, one for PSHE and Citizenship which are taken from the Key Stage 2 guidelines in the National Curriculum and the other for Thinking skills and other objectives. The thinking skills objectives are based on those outlined under 'Promoting skills across the curriculum' in the National Curriculum handbook.

Teacher's notes

Each activity or game then has an explanation of that activity or game and suggestions for how to introduce it to the children.

Plenary

This contains ideas for follow-up discussions and activities.

Photocopiable pages

These pages vary from a collection of cards to be cut out to a questionnaire for the children to complete. There are also some pages that contain a piece of text which is the basis for the activity or game but may not be intended for the children to have copies of.

Section

Bad behaviour?

Developing confidence and responsibility

PSHE and Citizenship objectives

- To talk about their opinions, and explain their views, on issues that affect themselves and society.
- To realise the consequences of anti-social and aggressive behaviour on individuals and communities.
- To know that their actions affect themselves and others, to care about other people's feelings and to try and see things from their point of view.

Thinking skills and other objectives

- To give reasons for opinions.
- To draw inferences and make deductions.
- To make judgements and decisions informed by reasons or evidence.

What you need

Photocopies of pages 7–9. Cut out each separate dialogue and list of questions. Glue them on to card.

What to do

- Explain to the children that you are going to tell them about an incident that happened at a school and that you want them to think about what should be done about it.
- Read out the following scenario:

  During the lunch break at St Phillip's School, three children were seen loitering around the headteacher's car. The headteacher, Mr Johnson, later found out that one of the headlamps on his car had been smashed. Each of the boys, together with a parent, is now waiting to see Mr Johnson.

- Ask for some volunteers to pretend to be each of the people waiting. Line up the seven volunteers, allocate roles and provide each of them with a copy of their dialogue. 'Introduce' each person to the rest of the class and ask them to read out their dialogue in turn.
- After each person has finished speaking the others might like to write down some questions they would like to discuss as a result of listening to the dialogue.
- After they have listened to each person's dialogue, ask the children to think about the following:

  Who do they think has behaved the worst? Give your reasons why.
  Who do they think has behaved the best? Give your reasons why.

  The children might like to discuss these questions in small groups and then feed back their ideas to the whole class.
- After this discussion, carry out a more in-depth discussion by referring to the children's questions written earlier as well as those on page 9. This discussion could be carried out in groups with each group considering a different set of questions – or with the class as a whole.

Plenary

Ask the children to tell you what they have learned from this activity. What do they consider the headteacher should do? Why? How might carrying out this activity help them in their own lives in the future?

Mr Johnson's headlamp

Mr Johnson

My name is Mr Johnson and I am the headteacher of the school. I will not tolerate this kind of behaviour any longer. I may have been lenient with these children in the past, but now is the time to be firm. We need much more discipline here and I intend to make an example of these three so that other people will be deterred from this kind of thing. I blame the parents. Children these days get too much freedom so the schools end up having to compensate for this. I don't expect any of them to admit to breaking my headlamp but I intend to punish all three to ensure the culprit gets what he deserves.

Iqbal Bassra

My name is Iqbal Bassra and I'm certainly not going to tell Mr Johnson who smashed his headlamp. I think friends should stick together, particularly against adults. I know that the other two would do the same for me if I'd done it. That's what friendship's all about in my opinion. It's important to be able to rely on each other at times like this. I don't really approve of lying, so I'll just refuse to answer any of their questions. That's not lying, is it?

Mrs Bassra

My name is Mrs Bassra and I'm Iqbal's mother. I'm really disgusted with his behaviour in this matter. He refuses to own up, but I'm certain he's the guilty one. My husband and I have tried to teach both our children high moral standards, but his sister has always been the more trustworthy in my opinion. I think it's only fair that Iqbal is punished by the headteacher and I expect my husband to punish him when he gets home from work whether he confesses or not. I feel that it is my duty as a parent to ensure that my children behave in a civilised manner and take my values as their own.

Luke Davies

My name is Luke Davies and yes, I did smash old Johnson's stupid headlamp. What's more, I'm glad I did it. He deserved it after all. He had no right to take away my cigarettes yesterday. I promised I would pay him back – and you should never break a promise, should you? Him and his big posh car – he thinks he's so wonderful. He's always picking on me and my mates so he needed to be taught a lesson. I'm certainly not going to own up. I'll probably say Mike did it. It's my word against his and Iqbal's but I can be much more convincing. Anyway, they know I'll get my mates to beat them up if they tell on me so I'm pretty safe. My dad believes me so old Johnson probably will too if he knows what's good for him.

Mr Johnson's headlamp

Mr Davies

My name is Mr Davies and I'm Luke's dad. It's disgraceful the way the headteacher has been carrying on about his headlamp. I've had to take time off work specially, even though it's perfectly obvious that Luke wasn't responsible. He says he didn't do it and that's good enough for me. That Mike looks like the ringleader as far as I'm concerned. I expect he comes from the council estate where this sort of thing is always happening. I certainly don't want my boy mixing with types like that but you can't really prevent it when they're in school, can you?

Mike Roberts

My name is Mike Roberts. I wish I'd managed to stop Luke from breaking Mr Johnson's headlamp, but I couldn't. He was determined to pay him back for confiscating his cigarettes yesterday. Just because I'm older than him doesn't mean that I can stop him from doing exactly what he wants. I really don't know what to say to the headteacher, but I suppose I'll tell the truth and hope for the best. I don't want to be the one responsible for getting Luke into trouble, but lying won't help him or any of us. I'll just tell them what happened and hope that the others will still talk to me afterwards. Luke's got some pretty nasty friends so I hope he won't get them to beat me up.

Mrs Roberts

My name is Mrs Roberts and I'm Michael's mother. Since he's the eldest of the three boys, I wouldn't blame Mr Johnson for holding him responsible. Whether or not he actually caused the damage is pretty irrelevant in my opinion. Surely he could have done something to prevent it? I'm amazed that he didn't just go and tell a teacher what was going on. The fact that he didn't makes me wonder if he was the one who did it, even though he swears he didn't. He's never liked Mr Johnson, so I wouldn't be at all surprised if it really was Mike.

Questions for discussion

Mr Johnson

- Has a headteacher the right to confiscate cigarettes from pupils?
- Will Mr Johnson be abusing his power if he punishes all three boys?
- Should Mr Johnson change his policy towards discipline merely because his own property has been damaged?
- Does punishment work as a deterrent?
- Should the innocent ever be punished?
- Does punishment benefit society, individuals or nobody?
- Are parents responsible for their children's behaviour – even in school?

Mr Davies and Luke

- Do two wrongs ever make a right?
- Is lying ever justified?
- Can we ever be certain that someone is not lying to us?
- How great a part does upbringing play in our current behaviour?
- Should we ever generalise about certain groups of people as Mr Davies does about people on council estates?
- Is it wise to keep children away from those whom we consider to be a bad influence on them?
- Why do you think Luke wants to lie?
- Are parents responsible for their children's behaviour – even in school?

Mrs Bassra and Iqbal

- Why do you think Mrs Bassra trusts Iqbal's sister more?
- Why do you think Iqbal thinks children should stick together against adults?
- Does friendship always mean sticking together regardless of the consequences or circumstances?
- Is refusing to answer questions a legitimate way to avoid lying?
- Should we take into account a person's past behaviour when judging present conduct?
- Who is ultimately responsible for a child's behaviour – parents, school or the child?
- Are parents responsible for their children's behaviour – even in school?

Mrs Roberts and Mike

- Should we always tell the truth regardless of the consequences?
- Should we ever be blamed for failing to act to prevent something terrible from happening?
- Should we be expected to 'tell tales' on our friends?
- Does age have any bearing on responsibility?
- Can we ever be sure that a person is truly responsible for their own actions?
- Why do you think Mike wants to tell the truth?

Section 1

What kind of person am I?

Developing confidence and responsibility

PSHE and Citizenship objectives

- To recognise their worth as individuals by identifying positive things about themselves and their achievements, seeing their mistakes, making amends and setting personal goals.

Thinking skills and other objectives

- To think carefully about themselves and their own worth.
- To give honest answers to personal questions.
- To consider personal change.

What you need

Photocopies of page 11, enough for each child to have one.

What to do

- Give each child a copy of page 11.
- Tell them that there are some statements to complete and that they should think very carefully before completing them. Explain that it is important they reply honestly.
- Reassure them that they can decide how much of the information they will share with others; they do not have to disclose any of it.
- The last part of the page contains an acrostic. If the children are not used to these, explain how they work. You could first work out a few as a class, perhaps using the name of a well-known television or film character, or sports personality.
- When the class have completed the questionnaire tell them they have a choice as to what to do next. They could:
  - sit quietly for a few minutes thinking privately about their answers before moving on to another topic without disclosing any information;
  - read their answers out to the class and ask for comments;
  - pass the papers around the class and guess who has written what;
  - disclose just one thing about him o herself;
  - ask their friends whether they agree with their answers to the penultimate statement.

They should put these options to the vote.

Plenary

Ask the children whether they feel the exercise has been valuable. Has it given them any 'food for thought'? Has it made them look differently at themselves or their friends? Discuss whether we see ourselves as others see us.

To share or not to share?

The three things I like best about myself are:

_____
_____
_____

The three things I like least about myself are:

_____
_____
_____

My greatest achievement so far is:

_____
_____
_____

The best thing anybody has ever said to me is:

_____
_____
_____

The person I'd most like to say sorry to is:

_____

If my friends were asked to describe me, they would say:

_____
_____
_____

In the future I hope to:

_____
_____
_____

Acrostic

Use the letters of your first name to begin some words that describe yourself, for example JANE.

JOLLY
AMIABLE
NUTTY
EVEN-TEMPERED

Facing challenges

Developing confidence and responsibility

PSHE and Citizenship objectives

- To face new challenges positively by making responsible choices and taking action.

Thinking skills and other objectives

Part One:

- To have practice in brainstorming.
- To think about the different ways of meeting a challenge.

Part Two:

- To differentiate between good and bad responses to a challenge.
- To discuss anonymous answers to questions objectively.
- To be able to amend and even refute one's own answers anonymously.

Part Three:

- To consider a number of challenges which may face or have faced them.

What you need

Photocopies of page 13, stuck on to card and cut out. You will need one challenge card for each group.

A4 or A3 paper.

What to do

Explain to the children that you are going to be talking about challenges. The session will be in three parts.

- Part One – On the board draw two columns, one headed 'Positive' and the other 'Negative'. Ask the children to brainstorm different feelings with which a challenge might be faced, for example scared, excited, reluctant, keen, enthusiastic, nervous and thoughtful. Ask the children under which column each suggestion should be written. Choose a scribe to write them on the board in the column agreed. Don't encourage any discussion as to why an answer should be in the positive or negative column or whether it should really be in that column.

- Part Two – Give everyone a piece of A4 or A3 paper and say that you are going to ask them a number of 'challenging' questions. Explain that they are to write down their answer to each question, folding the paper over after each one and passing it on to the next person. One word answers are not acceptable. When all the questions have been asked, each person is to unfold the paper they are holding and read out the answers for the group to discuss.

  - What exactly is a challenge?
  - What makes a challenge challenging?
  - How best should we respond to a challenge?
  - Are there any ways in which we should never respond to a challenge? Why/why not?
  - Are challenges always good? Why/why not?
  - Can we ever be too quick to accept new challenges? Why/why not?
  - What does the phrase 'He who hesitates is lost.' mean?
  - What does the phrase 'Fools rush in …' mean?
  - Which of the last two – to hesitate or to rush in – is more important when one is faced with a challenge?
  - Is our first reaction to a challenge likely to be the best? Why/why not?
  - Should we ever refuse to accept a challenge? Why/why not?
  - Do you need to be brave in order to face a new challenge? Why/why not?
  - If someone does something we consider to be dangerous, but has no fear, are they brave? Why/why not?

  Ask the children whether any of the words on the board should now be moved into the other column.

- Part Three – Divide the children into groups and give each group a photocopy of one of the challenges on page 13. One group member should read out the question to the others and be the scribe. The group should come up with suggestions for tackling the given challenge.

Plenary

The groups should join together to discuss their answers.

Challenges

You are soon to be moving house and will be going to a new school. You will need to make new friends both in the school and in your new neighbourhood. How will you face this challenge when you know nobody there except your own family? Think about any past experiences of moving house or school that you may have had.

You and two of your friends are the only ones from your class who have gone up to a particular secondary school. Your friends are both very unhappy there and want the three of you to stick together at all times. You know that it would be silly not to mix with the other children. They are already beginning to call your little group 'snobs' and you think that it will soon be too late to make any new friends. One or two children have tried to join your group, but your friends called them 'the enemy' and refused to be nice to them. How will you face this challenge without losing your old friends?

Members of your class have been offered the chance of a trip to France. You would like to go but don't want to ask your parents to pay for it because they can't really afford it. You know you will soon be learning French, so the visit could be valuable for you. How do you face the challenge of raising the money?

Your parents have promised you a really good present if you do well in all your schoolwork. You have done very well so far and know that your school report will be good, except for maths. You are really struggling with the subject. How will you face the challenge of improving your maths?

Your school is trying to raise money for some new computers. You've been told that the person who raises the most money will win some educational software for themselves. You think that the prize could really help you with your schoolwork. How do you face the challenge of raising money for the school without annoying the people you know by nagging them to give more than they want to, or by doing anything else unacceptable?

Do we need rules?

Preparing to play an active role as a citizen

PSHE and Citizenship objectives

- To understand why and how rules are made and enforced, why different rules are needed in different situations and how to take part in making and changing rules.

- To realise that by breaking rules we can endanger others and ourselves.

- To understand that insufficient or excessive rules can both be problematic.

- To realise that even law-abiding people are prepared to break rules sometimes depending upon the situation.

Thinking skills and other objectives

- Thoughtful examination of an important topic.

- To discuss with others who may have different views.

- To justify their own views.

- To back up statements with examples.

- To question the statements of others.

- To criticise a person's reasoning, not the person.

What you need

Photocopies of pages 15 and 16

What to do

- Tell the children that you are going to look at the problems that result from having too many rules or too few rules.

- Explain that you are going to read with them a piece of text about two lands, one called 'Freedom' and the other called 'Chains'. They have both been having problems with rules. Give the children copies of page 15 and then read it together.

- When you have read through the text and the laws, read through the questions on page 16, asking the children to give you answers as you read them out. It might be useful to record this part of the lesson so that you can revisit some of their thoughts later.

Plenary

Ask the children if they have learned anything from the exercise. Have they changed their views about rules and obedience?

Discuss school/classroom rules. How important are they? How important are punishments/consequences?

Freedom and Chains

A few years ago there were two neighbouring countries called Freedom and Chains. The ruler of Chains was very strict and was always passing new laws in an effort to keep the citizens under tighter and tighter control. In fact, there were so many rules in Chains that people didn't always realise when they were breaking them. With these laws being added to all the time, even the ruler couldn't remember all of them. Eventually the people of Chains began to get really angry about the rules and regulations they were now expected to follow. Life had been good in years gone by; they had been happy and prosperous and there had been little serious crime. They had come to believe that people were basically good, honest, fair and kind, but now they were feeling oppressed and nervous about doing anything in case there was a law against it. Life was becoming unbearable, so they decided to elect a new ruler who agreed to pass one more law, which said that all laws were to be abolished. The people were delighted and held an enormous celebration.

In Freedom, however, it was a different story. Their ruler was very lenient and there were hardly any laws. These people had begun to forget the difference between right and wrong and crime was on the increase. It wasn't called 'crime' of course, because almost any type of behaviour was now acceptable. The people were beginning to feel very unsafe and insecure. They couldn't trust anybody any longer. They felt that they no longer had any certainty in their lives. They constantly felt in danger and began to remember the 'good old days' when laws were there to be obeyed and people knew how to behave properly. Eventually, they decided that something should be done, so they elected a new ruler who said that he would introduce many new laws in order to stop the situation in Freedom from getting any worse. The people were delighted and held an enormous celebration.

NEW LAWS FOR THE PEOPLE OF FREEDOM

- You must never steal.
- You must never lie.
- You must never fight.
- Children must never disobey their parents.
- Teachers must always know all the answers.
- Everybody must exercise.
- You must never eat unhealthy food.
- Everybody must stay at school until they are 18.
- You must never drive faster than 30mph.
- Television is to be abolished.
- Everybody must have 12 hours' sleep each night.
- Everybody must pass all their exams.

There will be very severe punishment for all those who disobey.

Questions

- Can society as we know it exist without rules and laws?
- Do all societies, even primitive ones, live by rules?
- Is it possible to have too many rules?
- What is likely to happen in Chains now that they no longer have any laws?
- What will happen:
  - on the roads
  - in the shops
  - in the businesses
  - in the schools
  - in the homes
  - in the prisons
  - in the churches
  - in the government?
- Do you agree with some, none or all the laws for the people of Freedom?
- Do you agree that you should never steal? What if somebody is starving and will die without food?
- Do you agree that you should never lie? What if somebody is looking for your friend to harm him or her? Do you tell the attacker where your friend is?
- Do you agree that you should never fight? What if somebody attacks you?
- Should children ever disobey their parents?
- Should we believe everything teachers tell us?
- Is there anybody who shouldn't exercise?
- Is any food totally healthy or totally unhealthy?
- Should people be allowed to eat what they like?
- Should everybody be made to stay at school until they are 18?
- What would happen if we could never drive faster than 30mph? Would the roads be safer?
- Should television be abolished? What would be the result?
- Could you force everybody to have 12 hours' sleep? Would they be healthier if they did? Would there be any other consequences?
- Is there any way of ensuring that people pass all their exams?
- Should people be punished for breaking rules and laws?
- What sort of punishment would you recommend?
- Who should decide on the punishment and who should punish?
- What good does punishment do?
- Does punishment ever do real harm?
- Do two wrongs ever make a right?
- Should morals be a matter of personal choice or should we be told how to behave?
- What should we do if those in power bring in unfair laws?
- If we go abroad should we follow the laws of that country?
- How important is freedom?
- Are there any rules that you would like to see abolished?
- Are there any new rules you would like to see brought in?

Bullies, racists and friends

Preparing to play an active role as a citizen

What to do

- Put the photocopied question cards into a separate bag or box for each topic.
- Tell the children they are going to consider three very important topics – bullying, racism and friendship. (Or each issue could be considered separately in three different lessons.) Organise them into small groups and let them choose, or you choose for them, one of those topics for discussion. You might want to read out the questions to them before they decide.
- Explain to the children that they should take one question at a time and discuss it in their group. Specify a time limit for this. They should make notes about their discussion and decisions (or lack of decisions where relevant). One child may act as a scribe.
- Tell them that one word answers are unacceptable, but that it is not 'wrong' if they spend all the time discussing just one question, as long as they feel that the discussion is worthwhile.
- Only when they have discussed the question thoroughly should they take another question.
- Explain that they will be asked to feed back the results of their discussions to the whole group and that other children may comment and ask questions.

Plenary

Ask the children whether they found the exercise valuable. Have they learned anything about these important social issues that will make them act differently in the future? The combined efforts of the groups should hopefully give them a clearer picture of the nature of friendship, bullying and racism. By discussing the issues raised by the questions, the children will be peeling away layers of the topic, to get to the heart of it.

PSHE and Citizenship objectives

- To think about the nature of friendship and the serious issues of bullying and racism.
- To realise how harmful some behaviour can be.
- To try to understand why some people behave in an unacceptable manner.
- To consider ways of preventing bullying and racism.
- To consider change if they have personal tendencies towards bullying and/or racism.

Thinking skills and other objectives

- To discuss ethical issues in a small group situation.
- To give reasons for their views.
- To question the views of others.
- To amend their views as they gather evidence.

What you need

Photocopy the questions from pages 18–20 on to card and cut out individual questions.

Bullying

Do you consider bullying to be a serious problem?

Some people say that bullies are cowards. Do you agree?

How can you recognise a bully?

If bullies are people who force you to do something against your will, does that mean that parents, teachers and the police are bullies?

Are bullies always bad people?

Do bullies generally bully one particular person, or do they bully lots of people?

What would you do with people who are guilty of bullying?

What are the effects of bullying?

What can parents and schools do to deter bullies?

Which do you consider to be more damaging, physical or mental bullying?

Would it be a good idea to teach the person who is being bullied a martial art such as karate?

Do bullies also suffer by behaving in the way they do?

If somebody hits back at a bully, is that acceptable? Do two wrongs make a right?

Why do people bully one another?

Should you keep it secret if you are being bullied?

Is bullying usually between people of the same gender/age group, or of different gender/age groups?

What would you do if you were being bullied?

Racism

Is racism a serious problem in this country?

Is racism a problem even if no violence is involved?

How do you recognise a racist?

Why are some people racist?

Does racism run in families?

Is racism demonstrated in what people say, do, think, feel, or behave?

Is racism the result of fear, such as fear of the unknown?

Is racism always directed at minority groups?

Why do some people use violence against people of different races?

Do small children notice a difference between races?

If people of different races live near to one another and get to know one another, will there be more or less racial tension?

Is language a serious barrier to racial understanding?

Do some people use language to deliberately exclude others?

Should everybody speak the same language?

What is the most important difference between people of different races: colour, language, religion, culture or values?

Are people of all nationalities basically the same?

Should ethnic minorities be encouraged to blend into the new community or should they try to keep their own culture?

What can parents and schools do to stop racial tension?

Friendship

What is friendship?	How much do you need to know about one another before you can become friends?
How do you recognise a pair, or a group of friends?	Do people usually have friends who are similar to, or different from, themselves?
How do you know that someone is your friend?	What is the difference between a friend and a best friend?
What qualities do you look for in a friend?	Can friends dislike one another?
What is the difference between a friend and an acquaintance?	What keeps people friends even if they seldom see one another?
How do people become friends?	Can you have lots of close friends?
To have a friend, do you have to be a friend?	Can you make someone be your friend?
Can you be someone's friend without them being your friend?	Do people need friends like they need food and sleep?
Does friendship take time, or can it be instantaneous?	Should friends always be honest with one another?

Rights and responsibilities

Preparing to play an active role as a citizen

What to do

- Tell the children that they are going to play a game called 'In a spin'. Explain that the game is played with cards and dice and is about responsibilities, rights and duties at home, at school and in the community.
- Divide the children into groups of three or four and give each group the cards containing the three sets of questions.
- Explain that each person is to throw a dice and answer a question from the relevant group:

    1 and 2 = Responsibilities
    3 and 4 = Rights
    5 and 6 = Duties

  So, if someone throws a 5 they must take a card from the Duties pile.
- When that person has answered the question on the card, the other group members should contribute, and then move on to the next player when each has offered their suggestions.
- You (or an adult helper) should move from group to group, listening to suggestions and helping where necessary.

Plenary

Ask the children the following questions:
- Did you find the session valuable?
- Have you ever found yourself in any of the situations discussed?
- What part did you play in resolving the situation?
- How was the situation resolved?
- Do you think that you made the right choice?

PSHE and Citizenship objectives

- To think about their own responsibilities, rights and duties and also those of other people.
- To reconsider their attitudes towards ethical issues.
- To form strategies for dealing with awkward situations.
- To understand that sometimes their loyalties may lie in more than one direction.
- To understand that sometimes difficult choices must be made.

Thinking skills and other objectives

- To give reasons for opinions.
- To draw inferences and make deductions.
- To evaluate information.
- To consider the consequences of one's actions.

What you need

Photocopies of pages 22–24. You will need enough for one sheet per group. Mount the sheets on to card and cut out the sets of questions. If possible, give each set of cards a different coloured border, for example red for responsibilities, yellow for rights and blue for duties.

Dice.

In a spin

You have been looking after your neighbour's very badly behaved dog. Unfortunately it jumps over the fence and runs away. Is it your responsibility if it gets into further mischief?

The school field is covered with litter. The headmistress sends you all out to clear it up. Is the state of the school field everyone's responsibility?

Your friend says that she intends to pick some flowers out of her neighbour's garden to give to her mother on her birthday. Is it your responsibility to try to talk her out of it?

Your parents would like you to help on the farm during the summer, but you should be in school. Where does your responsibility lie?

Your mum insisted that you should look after your little sister while she made some important telephone calls, even though you said that you had to learn your spellings for the next day. But Mum still went into the other room to make the calls in peace and quiet. While you were busy concentrating on your work, your sister fell over and cut her leg. She wasn't badly hurt, but should your mum hold you responsible for the mishap?

In a spin

Your sister keeps coming into your room without knocking.
Do you have a right to privacy, or is there nothing you can do?

You were in the school toilets when two other children started splashing each other with water. A teacher caught them and has told the three of you to go to the headmaster. You told her that you were not involved but she wouldn't listen to you. Do you have the right to be heard?

The headmaster has wrongly accused you of being involved in a fight at school.
Do you have the right to be believed?

The chair in your bedroom has had a wobbly leg for weeks. You told your dad about it several times but he hasn't done anything about mending it. This morning the chair collapsed from under you and you hurt yourself. Do you have the right to be safe in your own home?

You have been saving your pocket money to buy the latest computer game but your parents think it is a waste of money and won't let you buy it. Do your parents have the right to stop you from spending your pocket money on what you choose?

A number of children in your neighbourhood keep taunting a homeless old man who is living locally. Although he has fallen upon hard times, does he still have the right to some respect from other people?

Your mother sometimes comes into your room and tidies it up for you. You have asked her not to bother, as you can never find anything afterwards and she sometimes throws out things that you want.
Have you the right to keep your room as you want it?

In a spin

You know that your friend has been playing in an area that is out of bounds. When a teacher asks if you know where he is, is your duty to tell the truth to the teacher or to protect your friend and warn him that the teacher has been asking questions?

Your friend asks you to lie for him. Is it your duty to refuse, or should you do as he asks because he is a friend?

You find a five pound note when walking home through the playground. Is it your duty to hand it in to a teacher or should you keep it?

Your friend asks if she can copy your homework. Should you let her, or is it your duty to refuse?

Your brother was involved in causing some damage at the school. The headmaster has asked if anybody knows anything about the people who did it. Is it your duty to tell, or should you protect your brother?

Your friend cheated in this week's spelling test. Should you keep quiet about it or is it your duty to tell somebody?

When it was your school's sports day one of your friends tripped somebody up during the long distance race. There were no other witnesses and your friend was awarded the first prize. Is it your duty to tell somebody or should you just leave it alone? After all, your friend may have won the race even without cheating.

Your mother expects you to help around the house even when you are busy with your homework. Sometimes you really can't spare the time to do the washing-up but she says it is your duty. Is she right?

Solving dilemmas

Preparing to play an active role as a citizen

What to do

- Tell the children that you are going to simulate a chat show called 'Problems PM' in which you, Di (or Dai) Lemma, are the host. Four children are needed to be the guests, preferably two boys and two girls. The rest of the class are to be the audience.
- Describe the format of the show. The first guest to be interviewed will be Kara. Then she will be joined, one at a time, by the others, starting with her father, Tony, her headmistress, Jane Davies, and finally Derek Williams, a businessman.
- Explain that you, as host, will question each of the guests in turn and that the guests may interact with one another. Members of the audience may comment and ask questions by raising their hands and being called upon by the host.
- Give each guest a photocopy of their own particular brief. Arrange suitable seating, with four chairs set aside for the guests, where they can be seen by members of the audience.
- Ask the guests to wait on one side until it is their turn to join the others on the 'stage'. They are able to listen from the 'wings' but not to contribute until they are called to the 'stage'.
- As the host you should facilitate the proceedings by introducing the discussion, enabling guests and audience to participate and drawing the discussion to a close by summing up any progress made and any future action to be taken.

Plenary

Ask the children whether they found the session valuable. Did the four guests enjoy their roles? Were members of the audience given sufficient opportunity to contribute? Was any solution reached? Was a compromise necessary?

Discuss how important it is to view all sides of an argument before being able to make an informed decision.

PSHE and Citizenship objectives

- To resolve differences by looking at alternatives, making decisions and explaining choices.
- To consider a problem from several angles.
- To understand the necessity for compromise.
- To see things from another person's viewpoint.

Thinking skills and other objectives

- To give reasons for opinions.
- To use precise language to explain what they think.
- To ask relevant questions.
- To give considered responses.
- To suggest hypotheses.
- To evaluate information.

What you need

Photocopies of pages 26–29.

Problems PM

"Well good afternoon ladies and gentlemen and welcome to 'Problems PM' with me, your host, Di (or Dai) Lemma. This afternoon we will be meeting a young lady called Kara. She has just taken her GCSEs and would like to stay on at school and then go to college. Also in the studio today is her father, Tony, who thinks that Kara should leave school now and get a job. He says he's not prepared to pay for her keep any longer. Kara's headmistress, Jane Davies, is also with us. She thinks that Kara has a bright future and should definitely go on to college after taking A levels, and finally Derek Williams is here. Derek is a representative of the community and has a business in town. As a parent Derek thinks that Kara should respect her father's views, but as an employer he believes that people like himself are looking for an educated workforce and would therefore like to see Kara leaving school with a number of valuable skills.

So those are our guests, but first, ladies and gentlemen, please welcome Kara." (CLAP)

Di (Dai) Lemma's possible questions to Kara

- Kara, why do you want to stay on at school?
- How many GCSEs did you take?
- So you're obviously a bright girl, but would you still have wanted to stay on if you hadn't been doing so well in your studies?
- Don't you think you should respect your father's decision? He's said 'No' so shouldn't that be the end of the matter?
- Why should your father be expected to keep you now that you are old enough to earn money yourself?
- Don't you care about your family's standard of living? Don't you care that your younger brothers are suffering from having a low standard of living?
- Wouldn't you rather have more money to spend on yourself, clothes, CDs and so on?
- You may think that you don't want to get stuck in a boring job, but can't all jobs be boring at times? This one may appear glamorous to you, but it can be really boring, believe me!
- Should we even expect to enjoy our job? Isn't work just something we have to do to earn money to live?
- That's all that your father is asking of you, that you go out and earn some money to live on. Is that too much to ask?
- Aren't the weekends meant for enjoying ourselves? Aren't they our reward for working hard at a tedious job all week?
- Is your real responsibility to your father or to yourself?
- What do you think your mother would have said if she'd been here today?

Problems PM

Di (Dai) Lemma's possible questions to Tony, Kara's dad

- Why don't you want Kara to stay on at school, Tony?
- Would it really cost so much to let her stay on? After all, it's only another couple of years we're talking about here.
- Just because you're unemployed, should Kara really have to give up her dream of having a career? Why should she be penalised for your misfortune?
- You said earlier that you want Kara's two brothers Ben and Jack to stay on at school. Is it fair that they will be allowed to stay on when she's expected to leave?
- Have you got something against educating women?
- Are you one of those people who think that women shouldn't even have the vote?
- Not all women get married or have babies, you know. The number of unmarried, childless women seems to be rising. Perhaps Kara will choose to be a career girl instead of a housewife. Wouldn't you feel that you'd let her down if she never married and never had a decent job because of your decision today?
- Do you think fathers are always right?
- If fathers are fallible, why should children always be expected to abide by what their fathers say?
- What do you think your wife would say about this?
- Should she be consulted?

Di (Dai) Lemma's possible questions to Jane Davies, Kara's headteacher

- Is Kara doing well at school?
- Is she generally a rebellious girl? After all, she's trying to go against her father's wishes, isn't she?
- Is the school prepared to take sides in this matter?
- Is it right for schools to take sides? Doesn't it just lead to more ill feeling?
- Do you think that you know better than the girl's father?
- Why do schools encourage their students to stay on? Is it just so that the school gets more money – more funding for themselves?
- Do schools really care about their students?
- Couldn't Kara leave school now and get a job and then, when things become a bit easier for the family financially, go on to the local college to sit A levels or GNVQs?
- Why should people be expected to get all their education over and done with straightaway? Isn't it better to wait until you're more mature?
- How would you feel if Kara stayed on for a while and then dropped out of the course? Surely her father would be angry if that happened?
- Kara hasn't had her GCSE results yet. I know she's expected to pass, but you can never be sure. What will you do if she fails?

Problems PM

Di (Dai) Lemma's possible questions to Derek Williams, a businessman

- I understand that you strongly believe that children should obey their parents. So what happens if each parent holds a different view? Doesn't it naturally follow that the child must disobey at least one of the parents?
- Perhaps Kara's mother would tell her to stay on at school if she was asked for her opinion. Would it be alright for Kara to stay on if her mother were to agree to it?
- Let's look at your other role, not as a father but as an employer. What sort of young people do you employ?
- So would you prefer to employ Kara as she is now, 16 years old, possibly with eight GCSEs (but that isn't guaranteed of course) or Kara as she will be in two years' time when she is 18 and probably has both GCSEs and A levels or GNVQs behind her?
- It's alright people saying there's no rush, she can always work now and study later, but don't you think it's difficult going back to being a poor student once you've got used to having a regular income?
- I expect some of your own employees are studying as well as working, so it's certainly not impossible to do both, but don't you agree that it must be hard for them to fit everything in? Doesn't their work begin to suffer if they're doing too much?
- Would you advise them to stop studying in that case, or to stop working?

Kara's brief

- You are 16 years old and have been doing well at school.
- You have just taken eight GCSEs.
- You would like to stay on and take A levels or GNVQs so that you can go to college.
- You would like to be a teacher eventually or maybe a nurse.
- Your parents are divorced and you and your two brothers live with your father who is currently unemployed.
- You are usually prepared to respect your father's views but are determined to have your own way on this occasion.
- You know that your father expects your brothers, Jack (15) and Ben (12) to stay on at school.
- You realise that he thinks education is wasted on girls because they just get married and have babies.
- With current high levels of unemployment, you realise that there is a great deal of competition for jobs, even low paid jobs, and want to give yourself a better chance.
- You are not prepared to take badly paid, boring work just to get money.

Problems PM

Tony's brief (Kara's father)

- You are a divorced father with three children. Kara is 16 and wants to stay on at school; Jack is 15 and Ben is 12.
- You are unemployed and would like Kara to start work right away to help with paying the bills that are mounting up.
- You think that a father's word should be law in the home and you are angry that Kara refuses to listen to you on this matter.
- You don't believe in careers for girls; they get married and have babies.
- You will want your two sons to stay on at school and get good jobs, but think that education is wasted on girls.
- Besides, when the time comes for decisions to be made about Jack and Ben's future, you may well have another job yourself. It's now you are thinking about, not some time in the future when money may be more plentiful.

Jane Davies's brief (Kara's headteacher)

- You are Kara's headmistress.
- You think Kara is a hardworking and intelligent pupil. She has taken eight GCSEs and is expected to pass them all well.
- You would very much like Kara to go into year 12 and eventually go on to college.
- You know that she would like to be a teacher or maybe a nurse and think she would be well-suited for either job.
- You strongly disagree with parents forcing their children down any particular avenue and believe that it is up to the child to make their own decisions.
- You had to face similar opposition when you were in school, but your own father eventually saw sense and is now very proud of your achievements.

Derek Williams's brief (A businessman)

- You are a father of a boy and a girl and own your own business.
- You believe that children should respect their parents' wishes.
- As an employer, you realise that key skills are often more highly valued in business than formal qualifications.
- When you are interviewing for workers, you look for those who 'understand the customer's requirements'; have command of 'basic IT skills'; have 'good communication skills' and who demonstrate 'the ability to learn'. You are also interested in those who have good numeracy skills and who are good at problem solving.
- You believe that, to be competitive, British businesses need a skilled, well-educated workforce.
- You admire both teachers and members of the nursing profession and think that, from what you have seen of Kara, she should make a good employee in one of the 'caring' professions.

Healthy or unhealthy?

Developing a healthy, safer lifestyle

PSHE and Citizenship objectives

- To differentiate between a healthy and unhealthy lifestyle and understand the benefits of exercise and healthy eating.

- To understand that making the 'right' choices is not always easy.

- To realise that we may be pressurised by other people and/or the media into choosing an unsuitable lifestyle.

Thinking skills and other objectives

- To give reasons for their opinions.

- To draw inferences and make deductions.

- To evaluate information and to judge the value of what they read, hear and do.

What you need

Photocopies of pages 31–33.

What to do

- Tell the children that they are going to look at what makes a healthy lifestyle.
- Ask them to make two lists, one of aspects of their own lifestyle that they consider to be 'healthy' and one of those which they consider to be 'unhealthy'.
- Put the children into groups and ask them to discuss their answers as a group. Suggest that each child thinks about whether there are any aspects of an unhealthy lifestyle that they are having difficulty in changing or giving up. Invite them to take it in turns to share any problems. Encourage other group members to offer suggestions and particularly to give examples of methods which they have found successful when trying to give up or change unhealthy habits.
- Stress the benefits of a healthy lifestyle and the disadvantages of an unhealthy lifestyle without resorting to propaganda or scaremongering.
- Now tell the children they are going to act out a role-play. Ask for volunteers to play the different roles. (If reading ability is a problem read the different parts out to them.)
- Hold a class discussion about the role-play and ask the children to answer the accompanying questions as appropriate.

Plenary

Ask the children if any of them found the session valuable. Has it made them more aware of the need to exercise and eat healthily? Will they do anything differently in future? If several of them have habits they would like to change, ask if it would be valuable for them to form a group in which members could offer one another support, advice and encouragement. Perhaps they could each keep a special diary in which to list their short- and long-term goals and also keep a note of their progress. Perhaps prizes could be offered as incentives.

Role-play

Girl: "It's not my fault that I'm fat. I'm big-boned, that's all. I can't do anything about it. It's no use exercising or eating less – Uncle Dave says it's genetic. I just take after him. But he's enormous! He actually makes me look tiny. Mum tells me not to eat so many sweets, but she doesn't understand. They cheer me up. I get really miserable sometimes. Some of the kids at school call me names. It's horrible. I need something to cheer me up when they're so nasty to me. My mum tries to make me eat salad but I just give it back to her. Rabbit food, Uncle Dave calls it.

My friends have started going to the leisure centre on a Saturday. They keep going on at me to go along, but you won't catch me in the swimming pool! I'd rather go to the cinema any day. I wish they'd all leave me alone and stop nagging."

Friend: "My friend is getting really fat. No matter what I say it doesn't make any difference. She won't stop eating sweets – it must be costing her a fortune. Goodness knows what it's doing to her teeth! She won't take any exercise. She never even bothers to turn up for games. Her mum refused to pick her up from school one day last week. She could easily have walked home but instead she phoned for a taxi! I couldn't believe it.

She used to be a bit chubby when I first knew her in primary school, but now she's really fat. Obese, my mum says. Some girls in my class don't like to be seen with her any more. They've started to call her names, but that just makes her worse. She gets depressed and then she eats even more rubbish. She won't come to the leisure centre with us on a Saturday and she always chooses the wrong things for school dinners. We learned what we should eat in our healthy living topic but she doesn't seem to care.

Her Uncle Dave's no help. He's fat too and he seems to encourage her. He probably feels better knowing he's not the only fat person in the family. I'm sure it can't be good for their health, let alone the fact that people are always making fun of them. It's bad for her physically and mentally in my opinion. I don't know how to help her if she won't help herself. She needs more willpower or something. I've even tried talking to the grocer where she buys her sweets about her, but he's just interested in his profits. I don't think there's anything else I can do."

Mother: "I'm getting really worried about my daughter. She's put on such a lot of weight recently. I try to encourage her to eat healthily but she never does. Her friends ask her to go to the leisure centre with them but she's too lazy. She won't even walk home from school and it's only round the corner.

She gets upset when people call her names and I hate seeing her miserable, but I suppose it's hardly surprising. She won't do anything to help herself. She's so negative.

Role-play

Dave doesn't help. He keeps saying that she's big-boned and takes after him. He says she can't do anything about it so she should ignore all the 'do-gooders' as he calls them and eat what she enjoys. I would have thought he'd have more sense, particularly after that health scare last year with his heart. The doctors warned him but he's just as bad as her. They just collude with one another and go out for a burger whenever he's over here. I'm actually quite ashamed of both of them."

Grocer: "I'm the owner of a small family grocer's and of course I try to stock the things that people want to buy. The other day I had this girl come in and tell me that I shouldn't sell sweets because they are bad for you. Honestly! Kids! She said her friend is always popping over here for sweets and crisps. I know the one she means. Tubby kid, likes the pick–'n–mix best. Yes, she's a bit overweight but I've seen plenty bigger than her.

But honestly, what a cheek of that other one to tell me I should refuse to serve her friend! I thought this was a free country. I expect she'll be back soon telling me to get rid of all the cigarettes and alcohol. I don't suppose she approves of me selling lard and full fat milk either. I ask you, is there any food that's 100% good for you nowadays? Even water can be polluted. Fruit and vegetables have got pesticides on them so they say, and even that organic stuff isn't perfect. Just horribly expensive. Look at beef, and people still want to buy that.

Perhaps that kid would like me to close down the shop completely. Anybody would think I could choose what to sell. If people don't want to buy organic artichokes or free range bantam eggs I'm certainly not going to stock them. Give me sweets and pop and crisps any day. You know where you stand with them. You know you've got a market for them. Besides, if I did close down or refuse to sell to her, she'd only go somewhere else. People in this country are supposed to have freedom of choice. Perhaps that young lady would like to go to a country where there's no freedom of choice and see just how much she likes it there. Honestly! Kids today! What would you do with them? They think they know everything.

I blame the schools. They fill their heads with all this healthy living nonsense and take all the fun out of life. Give me the good old days when full fat milk was good for you and cigarettes only stunted your growth. There was far less to worry about then. No wonder they're all anorexic nowadays. Nothing's safe to eat any more so they all want to starve themselves to be on the safe side. Glad I'm not a kid any longer. Far too stressful, I can tell you."

Questions

- Is the girl right when she says 'It's no use exercising or eating less' if you're 'big-boned'?

- Is it a good idea to eat sweets when we are miserable?

- Should people eat lots of salad? If so, why?

- Name some so-called 'healthy' foods.

- Is it good to exercise once a week at a leisure centre?

- Is all exercise good for you?

- What is 'aerobic' exercise?

- Should everyone be made to do games at school?

- Name some 'healthy' school dinners.

- Name some 'unhealthy' school dinners.

- Why is it bad for our health to be overweight?

- How can we summon up the willpower to eat healthily and exercise?

- Should shopkeepers take any responsibility for the food we eat?

- Should manufacturers be allowed to produce 'unhealthy' food?

- Should we be free to eat whatever we like?

- Should smoking, alcohol and/or 'unhealthy' food be banned?

- Should people take vitamins and other supplements?

- Should people be educated about living a healthy lifestyle? If so, how best can this be done?

- Should schools set an example by providing only 'healthy' dinners?

- Should television advertising of 'junk' food be banned?

- Who is responsible for children's eating habits – the parents, the schools, the media, the shopkeepers, the manufacturers, the farmers, the government or the children themselves?

- Do you think that most people in this country have a good diet?

Road safety

Developing a healthy, safer lifestyle

PSHE and Citizenship objectives

- To think about keeping ourselves healthy and safe.
- To recognise the different risks in different situations and then decide how to behave responsibly, including sensible road use.

Thinking skills and other objectives

- To listen carefully.
- To select relevant information.
- To remember relevant information.
- To work in small groups.
- To articulate opinions.
- To learn about road safety.

What you need

- Photocopiable pages 35 and 36.

What to do

- Tell the children that you are going to read them a text about road safety. Explain that the extract will demonstrate many of the dangerous ways in which some people behave in the street.
- Tell them that they should try to picture what is going on and to remember what is happening. They should listen particularly for any dangerous behaviour or hazards.
- Ask them to listen closely to what you have to say, but not to make any notes or comments.
- Read the road safety commentary on page 35 aloud to the class. (The numbers in the text refer to the list of possible road safety suggestions the children might make.)
- Organise the children into pairs or small groups. Ask them to list the dangers they heard about in the text. They should write what the characters did and also what they should have done.

Plenary

Bring the class together to discuss the result of the small group activity. Page 36 contains a list of points that the children might have suggested during their group work. Read through the list, asking who had made a note of each point as you do so. Do they agree with the list? Can they add anything to it?

Ask the children if they have learned anything about road safety that they didn't already know, or if the exercise has jogged their memory about anything they had forgotten. Ask about their own road safety and if there is anything that they will do differently in future.

Road safety commentary

"This is day one of our road safety campaign. It's a dark, miserable November morning and today we're focusing our secret video camera on the High Street where it runs in front of St Phillip's School. It's 8.55 and I have to say it's pretty chaotic here with late arrivals trying to get to registration on time.

The school buses have all left now but there are quite a few cars still pulling up on the double yellow lines outside the school (1) and dropping people off. Just five minutes to go before the bell.

There's one young man I recognise; it's Jo Evans, late as usual. He's wearing a black coat and a dark green bobble hat (2) (3). His bike really does need a clean; his reflectors are completely covered in mud (4). He's riding along the pavement (5) and he doesn't give any hand signals (6) before turning in at the school gates. Pity he didn't leave a bit earlier this morning.

Well, that's Jo in school. Now here's Surinder Soni. He's late as well, of course, and he knows it, so he's just dashed across the road (7) behind that parked van (8). If he'd looked both ways (9) or even taken the time to listen (10), he'd have known that there was a car coming. At least he's made it, this time. Ah, I see Jane Lewis is using the pelican crossing; now that's more sensible … or it would be if she'd actually waited for the green man. She's crossed while it's still the red man(11).

Now here's a group of half a dozen boys and girls. They're talking and laughing; they certainly don't seem to be concentrating on the traffic (12). They're not from this school; they're walking on past and round the corner. They aren't facing the oncoming traffic (13) and that side of the road doesn't even have a pavement (14).

I can see Mr Ganga bringing his little son Daljit to the crèche. Daljit is very near the edge of the kerb (15) and their dog is rushing about all over the place. I don't think he's got a lead on (16).

Marie Osborne's just arrived in her dad's car. I wonder if she's the last; it's almost 9 o'clock. She's opening the back door on the driver's side and is getting out into the road (17). No, she's not the last; here's Thomas Jones in his mum's car. No seat belt I see (18) and his baby sister Amy appears to be loose on the back seat too (19). Oh no, he's dropped his tennis ball and it's rolled into the road. I hope he's not going after it (20). Thank goodness for that; his mum's got it for him.

There, it's 9 o'clock and I can hear the school bell. I think a lot of people will be shocked when I play back this video. Don't you agree?"

Road safety suggestions

1. Only the disabled are allowed to park on double yellow lines.

2. Wear something light or reflective so that you can be seen.

3. Wear a cycle helmet.

4. Keep reflectors clean.

5. Don't ride along the pavement.

6. Always give the appropriate hand signals.

7. Don't ever run across roads.

8. Find a clear place to cross, not behind parked vehicles.

9. Always look both ways before crossing the road.

10. Always listen for traffic before crossing.

11. Only cross when the man is green.

12. Always be aware that roads are dangerous and be alert.

13. Walk facing oncoming traffic if there is no pavement.

14. Always use a pavement if possible.

15. Keep children away from the edge of the kerb.

16. Keep dogs on a lead.

17. Get out of the car onto the pavement rather than into the road if possible.

18. Always wear a seat belt.

19. Babies should travel in a special car seat.

20. If you drop anything in the road leave it or tell an adult.

Under pressure

Developing a healthy, safer lifestyle

What to do

- Tell the children that they are going to pretend to be an 'agony aunt' and try to work out some solutions to people's problems.
- Read out the letters to the agony aunt on pages 38 and 39. Organise the children into small groups and ask them to choose one of the letters to which to reply. Have ready several copies of each letter and give the groups their own copy.
- Tell the children their challenge is to try to offer advice to the writer of the letter. Tell them to avoid flippancy, embarrassment or being judgemental.
- One person in each group should be the scribe and will be required to feed back the advice offered when the groups join together.
- When the groups join together, members of other groups could take on the role of the person with the problem. They could articulate any difficulties or drawbacks they can see with the advice offered and make alternative suggestions.

Plenary

Ask the children if they found the activity valuable. Would any of the advice prove useful for anybody they know? Where do/would they go for help with any problems they might have?

PSHE and Citizenship objectives

- To explore the problems of peer and family pressures in a non-threatening, non-confrontational, non-judgemental environment.
- To relate the problems under consideration to any problems which they themselves may have and to hear the advice of their peers, without there being any need to admit to their own problems or to ask for help in dealing with them.
- To develop sympathy/empathy with others.
- To learn how to solve their own problems.

Thinking skills and other objectives

- To give considered advice to personal problems.
- To remain unbiased and non-judgemental, even when dealing with emotive issues.
- To understand the feelings and mindset of others.
- To realise that sometimes there is no ideal solution to problems.
- To realise that pressure exerted by others can be very hard to resist.

What you need

Several copies of pages 38 and 39.

Agony Aunt problems

Dear Agony Aunt,

I'm friends with a boy called Dave. A couple of weeks ago a new boy called Sam started at our school. He wears glasses and is a bit of a swot. Dave calls him teacher's pet because he always does his homework and gets good marks. Anyway, Dave really doesn't like Sam and the other day he decided to teach him a lesson. He found Sam's jacket and ripped it. Sam was very upset because it was a present from his dad. I didn't know whether to tell him it was Dave who did it or whether that would make things worse. Please help – I'm feeling really bad.

James

Dear Agony Aunt,

Every summer holiday I go with my family to a cottage in Wales. There isn't much to do there so I spend a lot of time with a group of kids from the village. The trouble is, they're always messing about on the railway line. I'm sure somebody is going to get hurt, but I don't know how to stop them. Can you give me some advice please?

Josh

Dear Agony Aunt,

My friend Lucy found £5 in the school field yesterday. I told her to take it to a teacher, but she said, why should she? The teacher would only keep it anyway and she needed it more than any of the teachers did. It must belong to somebody but Lucy doesn't care. She says she's going to spend it at the weekend. What can I do to make her feel guilty and hand it in?

Hannah

Agony Aunt problems

Dear Agony Aunt,

On Saturdays I always go to town with my mates. Last week Lee was complaining that he wanted a CD but he was broke. Des told him he should try to nick one because CDs are a rip-off in this country and the shops make too much profit anyway. Lee said he'd think about it. Now he's decided he'll give it a go next Saturday. I'm sure he'll get caught but he says he won't. What can I do?

Thomas

Dear Agony Aunt,

I live near a farm and the other day I went for a walk and saw a pony in their top field. It was in an awful state, thin and weak and covered in mud. It hobbled over to see if I'd got any food but it could hardly stand up. I took it some apples and carrots yesterday, but the farmer was working in the field. He shouted at me and told me to clear off. He said I was trespassing on his land and he'd get the police on to me. I wanted to tell the RSPCA about the pony, but then I'd be in trouble for trespassing. My dad says to leave well alone. What do you think? It's really upsetting me.

Carol

4
Section

It's not my fault!

Developing good relationships

What to do

- Tell the children they are going to role-play an event in which someone is hurt and that there are four different points of view about what happened and why.

- Copy and cut out the characters' role-plays and mount them on card. Ask for volunteers for the roles of the four characters concerned. They should each read their scripts in the order of Child, Granny, Father and then Mother.

- Discuss with the children their immediate reaction to the information they have been given. They should be asked to give one vote to the character who, in their opinion, is most at fault. The names of the characters should be written up and votes counted.

- The children should then be divided into four groups and assigned one of the characters. One person in the group can be scribe. Each person in the group should be given a copy of their character's script in order to refresh their memory of the events that have taken place. They should be encouraged to think about the problem for themselves, but can be given the accompanying questions as prompts. The aims are:

  (1) to decide what their character should have done in order to avoid the mishap

  (2) to write a minimum of three New Year's resolutions for their character, for example for the child 'I will not be so untidy in future; I will not be cheeky; I will be more thoughtful.'

Plenary

Ask the groups to come together to share their findings. Having discussed the situation in greater depth, have they changed their opinion as to who was at greatest fault? Should any action be taken?

Ask whether they believe either or both of the following people to be guilty of something: the man who deliberately aims a gun at someone but misses the shot and causes no harm; or the man who shoots another person by mistake. If they are guilty, what are they guilty of and should they be punished?

Characters

Child

It's not my fault Granny fell over my truck and hurt her leg. How was I supposed to know she'd left her glasses in the sitting room? I'm always allowed to play in there and I need plenty of room when I've got my garage out. Anyway, I thought Granny was having a nap upstairs. It couldn't have been my fault when I thought she was upstairs. She could have asked somebody else to get her glasses for her. She knows she's a bit wobbly on her feet. She was asking for trouble trying to walk over my road mat. Anyone can see it's slippery. She must have seen the truck – it's red after all. Anybody could have seen it. I know she hadn't got her glasses on but it's huge. She didn't have to fall over it.

She probably did it on purpose to get some attention. Everybody was busy and she wanted somebody to take notice of her. They certainly started to take notice of her then. I'm sure she didn't have to cry so loudly. She really scared me. It couldn't have hurt that much. Besides, she soon quietened down when everyone made a fuss of her. She was really cross with me, but Mum said it was Dad's fault for not telling me to tidy up. Dad said it was Mum's fault for not checking that I'd done it, but I still think it's Granny's own fault. She's a grown-up after all. She's always telling me to be careful of everything – she should have been more careful herself.

Granny

My leg still hurts after falling over that truck. They're far too soft with that lad in my opinion. It's all his fault that I'm in such pain. His parents haven't even punished him. It's as if he can do no wrong. He's so untidy, I'm surprised there aren't more accidents in this house. They never seem to discipline him. He does just what he wants. His father was never allowed to behave this badly when he was that age. I don't imagine his mother was either. No wonder the children today are so naughty if their parents refuse to smack them. They haven't even sent him to his room. I don't think he actually knows the difference between right and wrong yet. He even had the cheek to

say it was my own fault! Fancy saying that to a grown-up! He said I should have known I'd fall over something.
Why on earth did he think I was going to get my glasses if I could see properly without them? He may think his truck is easy to see but I didn't see it without my glasses. Does he think I fell over on purpose? His mother blames his father for not telling the lad to tidy up before lunch and his father blames his mother for not checking, but I know that it's the child's fault – he's quite old enough to take responsibility for himself without his parents having to do everything for him. He's not a baby any more; he should know better than to leave things lying about.

Characters

Father

My mother does tend to overreact sometimes. I know she's had a nasty fall, but there's nothing broken and she soon calmed down after a cup of tea. She was sitting with her leg up for a while but she's walking around quite happily now. No real harm's been done. I know she hates untidiness – I was never allowed to bring my toys out of my room when I was little. Her house is spotless and you don't dare make a dent in the cushions, but when she comes here she has to take us as she finds us. She has to realise that we don't share her values. We don't mind a few toys around the place. At least it makes it look lived in, not a show house like hers. People always feel uncomfortable at her house, but our friends can relax when they come here.

My wife asked me to tell the boy to tidy up before lunch because the Bradleys are coming later and I did tell him. Admittedly I called through the door to him on my way to answer the phone, but how was I to know if he'd heard me or not? It's her own fault for not checking that he'd done it. She asked me to tell him and I told him. It's not my fault if he didn't hear. If the Bradleys are so fussy she should have done the tidying up herself, or at least supervised while he did it. She knows I wouldn't have bothered tidying up for them. It only encourages them to come round and I'd rather they didn't bother. They should go round to my mother's house if they want pristine conditions.

Mother

Right, that's the washing-up done. The Bradleys will be here soon so I'd better finish tidying the sitting room. Granny seems a lot more cheerful now after her little mishap this morning. Poor dear, she is getting quite frail. It's all my husband's fault. I told him to make sure the sitting room was tidied up for the Bradleys, but of course he didn't do it. Calling through the door's no good; he should have gone right in. He's always cutting corners; never does anything properly. Now look at his mother. It's his fault she's had a nasty shock. He lets our son get away with anything. If I try to discipline him, his father tells me not to be so fussy. He even blames me for his mother's mishap this morning.

He says I should have checked that the room was tidy. Honestly! I was in the middle of making the lunch. He's the one who grumbles if the custard's lumpy – I could hardly leave it. Besides, I'd asked him and that was enough as far as I'm concerned. I know he doesn't like the Bradleys, he probably wanted the sitting room to be untidy when they arrived. He probably hoped one of them would fall over the toys – that's just the way his mind would work. He's always telling me to delegate when I'm busy at the office. If I try to delegate here for once, look what happens. It's his own fault his mother's in pain. He certainly can't blame me for that.

Questions

Child

- Does it make any difference whether the child knew that Granny had left her glasses in the sitting room?
- Does it make any difference that he's always allowed to play with his toys in there?
- Is he right when he says 'It couldn't have been my fault when I thought she was upstairs'?
- If someone knows that they are a bit wobbly on their feet, should they be blamed for trying to do something for themselves?
- Should we do things for people even if they don't want us to?
- Do people ever really 'ask for trouble'?
- Just because the child knows that the mat is slippery, can he be sure that everyone else can see that it's slippery?
- Can the child be sure that his grandmother saw the truck?
- Would somebody really fall over something on purpose to get attention?
- Can we ever know how much pain somebody is feeling?
- Should adults offer advice to children if they don't take it themselves?
- Should children always listen to the advice of adults?
- Do adults necessarily know more than children?
- Do you think that the child heard his father telling him to tidy up?
- Can we ever know all the consequences of our actions?
- Is it the child's fault that Granny fell over?

Granny

- Should the child have been punished by his parents?
- What exactly did he do wrong?
- Did he do anything wrong if he hadn't heard his father telling him to tidy up?
- Are children who aren't disciplined always naughtier than those who are?
- Should parents ever smack their children?
- Is sending a child to their room always an effective punishment?
- Is punishment a good thing?
- Why don't adults like children to be cheeky to them?
- How do children learn the difference between right and wrong?
- At what age should children be expected to know the difference between right and wrong?
- Whose values do children usually choose?
- When should parents stop taking responsibility for their children?
- If children are naughty, whose fault is it?
- Is it Granny's own fault that she fell over?

Questions

Father

- How can we judge that someone is overreacting?
- Can the father know that no real harm's been done, just because his mother is walking around again now?
- Did Granny have to break something for real harm to have been done?
- Why do some people hate untidiness?
- Is it better to be really tidy or really untidy?
- Is tidiness an important value?
- What values do you consider to be important?
- Can parents and children usually see things from one another's point of view?
- Did the father do as he was asked by calling to the boy through the door?
- Was it his fault if the boy didn't hear him?
- Should the boy's mother have been expected to check up on them?
- If we don't check, is it our fault or theirs if things don't get done?
- Should we tidy up before people come or should they take us as they find us?
- Will people think any less of us if they see us as we really are?
- Is it the father's fault that Granny fell over?

Mother

- Should the wife be the one who does the cooking and the washing-up?
- Are old people always frail?
- If the father generally doesn't do things properly, can we assume that he hasn't done things properly this time?
- Can we ever be sure that somebody is telling us the truth?
- If we keep telling people that they are lazy or unreliable or naughty, will that make them even more lazy, unreliable or naughty?
- How can parents discipline their children if they both have different values?
- Do you think that the father wanted one of the Bradleys to fall over the toys?
- If somebody feels guilty, does that mean that they are guilty?
- When should we delegate work?
- Is delegating work always a good idea or are we shirking our responsibility?
- Why does the mother want to tidy up before the Bradleys come?
- Should people always be believed to be innocent until they are proved guilty?
- Is it the mother's fault that Granny fell over?

Different ways of life

Developing good relationships

What to do

- Tell the children that they are going to find out about how people live in different countries.
- Ask for volunteers to read the 'Foreign lands role-plays' to the class.
- Explain to the children that they should listen carefully without making notes as they will be asked questions straight after the readings.
- Organise the children into small groups and give each group a copy of the questions on page 50. They should write down the answers to the questions as quickly and as accurately as possible. One point will be awarded for each correct answer (provided in page 51) and the winners are the group with the highest score.
- Groups should feed back their answers verbally to the whole class for scoring purposes.

Plenary

Did the children find the session valuable? Do they know many foreign people personally? Why is it important to learn about other people and places? How can it help our own lives?

PSHE and Citizenship objectives

- To understand that different peoples may share some of their customs and values with other races, while some customs and values may be unique to them.
- To realise that much racial tension comes from a fear of the unknown and a subsequent lack of understanding of other people.
- To consider the possibility that 'familiarity' may lead to 'fondness' when it comes to learning about people from different countries.

Thinking skills and other objectives

- To exercise their powers of memory.
- To extract relevant information from spoken text.
- To evaluate information.
- To co-operate and share with others in a small group situation.

What you need

Photocopies of pages 46–51.

Foreign lands role-play

India

My name is Usha and I am an Indian girl. My family is quite large; I have four brothers and three sisters altogether. We live with our parents and grandparents and nearby live many of our aunties, uncles and cousins. We have great respect for older people here and also for our father, who is the head of the family. All family members in India are very dependent upon one another.

Marriage is extremely important to Indians. My sister will soon be getting married and I will have a new sari for the occasion. We still have many arranged marriages in India. Usually the bride and groom have not even met before the wedding, although sometimes they may have exchanged photographs, or they may have met briefly as part of a large group. Occasionally there are 'arranged love marriages', for example when the bride and groom have fallen in love at college, but this is not usual. People sometimes put adverts in the paper when trying to arrange a marriage for their offspring. It can be quite hard work.

The groom's family expects to receive a good dowry from the bride's family. The married couple will then go and live with the groom's family. Babies are very welcome when they arrive, particularly boy babies and children are often very pampered for the first few years of their life. Unfortunately, there is still some child labour in my country, so not all children here are able to go to school, particularly those from poor families, who must work from an early age.

There are several traditional decorations that Indian women wear as well as the sari. You may have seen the 'bindi' or the 'tilak', the red dot that is on their forehead. You may also have noticed the nose-ring that is worn by Muslim brides or the nose-pins and bangles that Indian women often wear. These each have their own story, and are very important customs for us.

In the south of India, where I live, rice is a staple food. We also enjoy very spicy food here and are famous for our curries. Mealtimes are very important to us and we like to share our food with guests. Food also plays a large part in our festivals and celebrations. You may have heard of Diwali, the Festival of Lights. It is celebrated by Indians all over the world. There is feasting and we let off firecrackers and light lamps. Diwali is celebrated for five days and marks the beginning of the Hindu New Year.

There are many different religions in India, although the majority of people are Hindu. There are rules about what people are allowed, or not allowed, to eat. Hindus will not eat beef or use leather because they believe that cows are sacred. The Islam religion forbids Muslims to eat pork or drink alcohol. You will also find here Christianity, Sikhism, Buddhism and Jainism. Our official languages are Hindi and English.

    PSHE and CITIZENSHIP activities

Foreign lands role-play

Spain

My name is Maria and I come from Spain. I would like to tell you a little about my country. The main language here is Castilian Spanish. That is what I speak. You may have heard of our best-known cities – Madrid and Barcelona.

We are very fond of our food in Spain. We have a Mediterranean diet, which is considered to be very good for us. We use plenty of garlic and olive oil in our cooking and eat lots of fruit and vegetables. After lunch, the shops and businesses close so that people can take a siesta. That is when we rest. Lunch is our main meal and paella is probably the best-known Spanish dish.

Not everybody approves of bullfighting, but here in Spain it is still very popular. The bullfighters, or matadors, are even considered to be heroes by many people in this country.

Almost all Spanish people are Roman Catholic and we have many fiestas (or festivals) to celebrate our saints' days. Every town and city has its own patron saint. One of my favourite celebrations is San Antonio's day, which takes place on January the 17th. Some people light bonfires on that day, while others take their animals to be blessed by San Antonio. It is a really good time for us.

I must tell you about Christmas in Spain. The festivities last for several days, not just the 25th and the 26th of December. On December the 24th we have a very special family meal and then we go to church. After Christmas, on December the 28th people play practical jokes on one another and then on New Year's Eve there is another family celebration. Some people nowadays have a tradition that, when it is midnight, they eat a grape for each strike of the clock, followed by a glass of sparkling wine. They then go to parties, coming home the following morning for another family meal. The Spanish have good fun over Christmas and New Year.

We also love music and dancing and probably the best-known Spanish music is flamenco. Tourism is very important for our economy nowadays. Many people from countries such as yours come to Spain each year. They really enjoy our good climate and good food.

Foreign lands role-play

Russia

My name is Ivan and I come from Russia. I live in a three room flat with my parents, my grandparents, my brother Igor and my sisters, Olga and Nikita. Families here are very dependent upon one another, living together in flats as many of us do. Both my parents go out to work. They have to commute into the city by bus because cars are still quite a luxury here and we do not have one.

We have a lot of celebrations here in Russia. One that is very important is International Women's Day on March the 8th. It is a national holiday and all the women are treated as special. Men give them gifts and flowers and even do the housework for them. In Russia we really enjoy celebrations. My favourite is definitely New Year. This is the best Russian holiday. It is when Grandfather Frost brings our presents. The Snowmaiden helps him. It is then that we have a tree with bells and decorations. The Russian Orthodox Church celebrates Christmas on January the 7th, although the Catholic Christmas is celebrated on the 25th of December as it is in your country.

We must be careful of the water here in Russia, some of it is unfit to drink. We enjoy strong tea and vodka is often used for people to toast one another at mealtimes. We eat dark, heavy bread, which is nothing like your soft bread in Britain. In my house we have a big cooked breakfast in the morning, although some people just have a sandwich and tea or coffee. We have our dinner at about 1pm. This is our main meal of the day, with food like soup, pickles, smoked fish and a dessert too. Between dinner and the evening meal children and older people usually have a snack and a nap.

You have probably heard of some of our famous Russian foods. Borscht is a beetroot soup. Then of course there is caviar and beef stroganoff, and pancakes called blini are also very popular here. I particularly enjoy drinking lemon tea. We do not use convenience foods in my family because they are too expensive.

In the evenings I enjoy watching TV and reading. Books are cheap here in Russia, so I am able to buy plenty of them. We don't eat out or anything like that because it is far too expensive, so we spend the evenings together as a family.

Because both parents usually work, children can go to pre-school until they are about six or seven years old. Although our schools are often overcrowded and do not always have good facilities, we still greatly respect our teachers in Russia and believe that education is very important. I hope to go to university eventually and maybe become a doctor.

Foreign lands role-play

Japan

My name is Takeshi and I am a Japanese boy. Now what can I tell you about my country? When people think of the Japanese people they think of men in smart suits and women wearing the kimono. You will not see many women wearing a kimono nowadays because they are very expensive and are generally kept for special occasions such as weddings and New Year. We like to wear jeans and t-shirts, but we never wear outdoor shoes in the house. We take them off at the door and put on slippers, but even these must be taken off in the 'tatami' room, which has a delicate rush floor.

People think that some of the food we eat here is pretty unusual. We have sushi, which is often made with raw fish; eels; seaweed; octopus; venison and horse, as well as the usual western types of food. Of course we also use chopsticks, which some westerners find difficult to cope with. We use disposable chopsticks in restaurants. When people think of a Japanese meal they will usually think of rice and they'd be right to do so, because we serve it with every meal. Although I enjoy toast and coffee for my breakfast, my parents and grandparents have boiled rice, miso soup and pickled vegetables. We enjoy very good health here in Japan so our diet cannot be too bad for us, even if it is considered unusual by some westerners. Nowadays the young people here also like fast food, as they do in Britain and the US.

Our school year starts on April the 1st and ends March the 31st. We must attend from Monday to Friday and also half day on Saturday. We study many subjects including music, art, the Japanese language, haiku (Japanese poetry) and calligraphy, which is the art of writing. Japanese students work very hard to achieve good results. We are particularly good at mathematics in this country.

My father works long hours and commutes to work, but my mother stays at home to look after the family. On Sundays we all go on outings as a family. In our spare time we watch TV. We are also very keen on reading. We depend on one another as a family.

There are two main religions in Japan. Those who have the Shinto religion believe that there are spirits in everything, even water and rocks. The Buddhists believe that everybody comes back again in another form or as a different person.

There are some Japanese activities you may have heard of. Our tea ceremony is often a talking-point with foreigners and many people know of bonsai, which is the growing of miniature trees, and origami, or paper folding.

You may find it interesting to learn about bath time in Japan. First of all we shower ourselves clean and then we soak in a tub. This means that we can all share the tub water because it is still clean. I don't think you do this in Britain.

Foreign lands questions

1. Grandfather 'Who?', comes to Russia at New Year?

2. What is another word for a Spanish festival?

3. Which country is famous for flamenco music?

4. Name three religions practised in India.

5. When does the school year start in Japan?

6. What is a staple food in the south of India?

7. What is the Spanish word for a bullfighter?

8. When do Orthodox Russians celebrate Christmas?

9. Which is the main meal of the day in Spain?

10. What animal is sacred to Hindus?

11. What do Russians celebrate on March the 8th?

12. Which Indian religion does not allow people to eat pork?

13. Name the two main religions in Japan.

14. Which is the best-known Spanish dish?

15. In which country do they have arranged marriages?

16. What is calligraphy?

17. When do Japanese women wear a kimono nowadays?

18. What are blini?

19. What religion are most Spaniards?

20. What do Japanese families do on Sundays?

21. How long does Diwali last?

22. Describe Russian bread.

23. Explain the Japanese bath time routine.

Foreign lands answers

1. Grandfather 'Who?', comes to Russia at New Year? (Frost)

2. What is another word for a Spanish festival? (Fiesta)

3. Which country is famous for flamenco music? (Spain)

4. Name three religions practised in India (Buddhism, Sikhism, Hinduism, Islam, Jainism and Christianity)

5. When does the school year start in Japan? (April the 1st)

6. What is a staple food in the south of India? (Rice)

7. What is the Spanish word for a bullfighter? (Matador)

8. When do Orthodox Russians celebrate Christmas? (January the 7th)

9. Which is the main meal of the day in Spain? (Lunch)

10. What animal is sacred to Hindus? (Cow)

11. What do Russians celebrate on March the 8th? (International Women's Day)

12. Which Indian religion does not allow people to eat pork? (Islam)

13. Name the two main religions in Japan. (Shinto and Buddhism)

14. Which is the best-known Spanish dish? (Paella)

15. In which country do they have arranged marriages? (India)

16. What is calligraphy? (The art of writing)

17. When do Japanese women wear a kimono nowadays? (Special occasions)

18. What are blini? (Russian pancakes)

19. What religion are most Spaniards? (Roman Catholic)

20. What do Japanese families do on Sundays? (Go on outings)

21. How long does Diwali last? (Five days)

22. Describe Russian bread. (Dark and heavy)

23. Explain the Japanese bath-time routine. (A shower followed by a soak)

Interviews

Developing good relationships

PSHE and Citizenship objectives

- To consider the meaning of the term 'family'.
- To look at their own relationships with other people.
- To think about family life from the point of view of others as well as themselves, for example that of a parent or someone from another country.
- To look at both the good and the bad sides of family life.
- To examine differences between the relationship they have with their friends and the relationship with their family.
- To consider the extent to which family members can also be friends.

Thinking skills and other objectives

- To develop questioning skills.
- To improve listening skills.
- To develop summarising skills.
- To improve note-taking and writing skills.
- To improve memory.
- To develop a specific style of writing.

What you need

The two sets of questions from pages 54 and 55.
Pens, pencils and paper.
Examples of interviews with celebrities from magazines or newspapers.

What to do

- Tell the children that they are going to work in pairs to interview each other about their relationships with their families and others. Talk about the types of articles to be found in the media where celebrities have been interviewed. If possible, read some of them out. You could use the two examples on the opposite page. Look at the style of writing used.

- Talk about journalists and how they have to make notes when interviewing someone. How would they do this? Although some use shorthand, these days many do not and have to use other devices such as key words or mind maps. Write some examples of both on the board.

- Now split the children up into pairs. Make sure that everyone has paper and pen or pencil. Explain that each person in the pair will be given a set of questions. One of them will have the set about relationships and the other the set about families. They are to interview each other, using the questions, asking for their views on the subject. They may need to make notes as they go, to remind them what has been said. Emphasise that the notes should be brief and remind them about the use of key words and mind maps.

- From time to time, the person who is interviewing should summarise what has been said in order to check that he or she has understood properly.

- When the interviews are finished, tell the children that they are now to write their interviews in the style of a magazine or newspaper article. Explain how long the article should be and decide whether they should add a drawing of the interviewee in lieu of a photograph.

Plenary

The children could either read out their articles to the whole class or pass them round for comment. They could finally be typed up and collated.

Each person should say whether their views were properly presented in the article or whether the interviewer misunderstood them.

Discuss the importance of listening carefully, answering questions succinctly and saying exactly what you mean.

Examples for interviews

JADE KENNEDY BELIEVES THAT THE WORST THING ABOUT FAMILY LIFE IS BOSSY SISTERS!

When I interviewed Jade Kennedy earlier today she told me that, in her opinion, a family is a group of people who live together. 'They don't have to be related,' said Jade, 'but it's nice if they are.'

She went on to tell me that the best things about her family life are her dad's cooking and her cat, Robinson. Jade has a brother, Tom, and a sister, Laura. Jade thinks this is the ideal size for a family, even though she described her sister as 'extremely bossy'.

'I CAN'T COUNT THE NUMBER OF DIFFERENT ROLES I PLAY.'

Ben Anderson says the list of roles is almost endless: son, brother, nephew, pupil, neighbour, customer – he soon lost count.

'I behave differently with everybody,' Ben told me. When I asked him why, he said 'My mum would have a fit if I talked to her the way I talk to my mates and they'd think I was crazy if I acted like I do when I go to see my grandparents. They're very strict, so I have to be polite in their house.'

I asked Ben why he thought we behaved differently with different people. 'It's probably something to do with respect,' he said. 'But your mates prefer to see you as you really are.'

Questions about families

What is a family?	What are the best things about family life?
What are the worst things about family life?	Do children who are brought up in children's homes have a family?
Are children who have been brought up in a children's home capable of adapting to family life?	Is family life desirable?
When should people start a family?	What is the ideal family size?
Are two parents better than one?	In China people are only allowed to have one child. What do you think about this?
In France people have been rewarded if they have a fifth child. What do you think about this?	Can a parent and child ever be best friends?
Do parents always know better than their children?	Should children ever be taken away from their families?
Should we be loyal to our family?	Should unborn babies be screened for imperfections?
What does the expression 'blood is thicker than water' mean?	Should anybody be prevented from fostering/adopting children?
Should anybody be prevented from having children?	Should people of one culture be allowed to adopt children of another culture?
Should we obey our parents?	

Questions about relationships

If we don't like somebody should we tell them?	If we have a bad relationship with our parents are we likely to have a bad relationship with our children?
Why are teenagers often rebellious?	How much freedom should children be given?
Now that people are considered to be adults at eighteen, should they still be expected to go to school?	Can girls and boys be friends without being girlfriend and boyfriend?
At what age should youngsters be allowed to date?	What qualities do girls look for in boys?
What qualities do boys look for in girls?	Do our parents look for the same qualities in our friends as we do?
Do parents always want what is best for their children?	Do children always want their parents to be proud of them?
Should we worry if we don't get on well with our brothers and sisters?	Is marriage becoming more or less popular?
Which relationship is generally considered to be the most important?	Do we need relationships with other people or could we exist in total isolation?
How many different roles do you have? (Daughter/son/brother/sister/aunt/uncle/friend/pupil)	Why do we behave differently with different people?

4
Section

Stereotyping
Developing good relationships

PSHE and Citizenship objectives

- To understand what stereotyping is.
- To realise that stereotyping can be both harmful and offensive.

Thinking skills and other objectives

- To think critically about their own experiences of stereotyping and being stereotyped.
- To generate more accurate ways of describing groups of people.
- To understand that very few generalisations may legitimately be made about groups of people.

What you need

Photocopies of pages 57–60.

What to do

- Ask the children what they understand by the term 'stereotype'. Explain that it is to do with making generalisations about different types of people and having fixed, often unjustified, ideas about them.
- Explain that stereotypes do not just relate to different races, they can be used about anyone with regard to their gender, religion, age, family background, school – in fact anything that makes people different from one another. (For example, 'All children from St Phillip's School are snobs.') Suggest that we are most likely to stereotype people that we don't know personally.
- Hand out photocopies of 'Mix and match' and explain that six descriptive words are needed for each.
- Ask the children to fill in their answers in pairs and then feed back to the class.
- Hand out photocopies of the 'Stereotypes' sheet and ask the children to tick all the boxes that apply to them before completing the final statement. They may not want to share their answers to the first two statements, but should be encouraged to share their answers to the third.
- Explain that stereotypes are counterproductive because they are often false, which means that once we have the wrong impression of someone, it can be very difficult for us to change our mind about them. Stereotyping people can also be very offensive to them. It can lead to a 'self-fulfilling prophecy' in which people begin to live up to (or more often, down to) public opinion of them. If, for example, a particular race of people is considered to be dishonest, a member of that race may see no point in being honest himself, since he is always considered to be suspect.
- Hand out photocopies of the 'All … All …' sheet. Explain that this contains some familiar stereotypes. Split the children into small groups to come up with accurate descriptions of the people being described – that is a statement that is not a stereotype but a true fact. Tell the children that a point will be given for each correct answer and that two points will be given for a correct answer that no other group has. Groups should feed back their answers and receive their scores. If you feel assistance is needed some possible answers are on page 60.

Plenary

Can the children think of examples of stereotyping in the newspapers, magazines, television or films? How do they think stereotyping can be avoided?

Mix and match

Below is a list of people who are sometimes stereotyped. Find six words for each that you think describe each person.

Teacher

_____   _____   _____

_____   _____   _____

Police officer

_____   _____   _____

_____   _____   _____

Nurse

_____   _____   _____

_____   _____   _____

Soldier

_____   _____   _____

_____   _____   _____

Criminal

_____   _____   _____

_____   _____   _____

Teenager

_____   _____   _____

_____   _____   _____

Stereotypes

I would be most likely to stereotype people who are of a different:

RACE ☐

GENDER ☐

AGE ☐

BACKGROUND ☐

RELIGION ☐

NONE OF THESE ☐

I have been stereotyped by other people because of my:

RACE ☐

GENDER ☐

AGE ☐

BACKGROUND ☐

RELIGION ☐

NONE OF THESE ☐

Stereotyping is wrong because:

_____

_____

_____

_____

All ... All ...

All girls are gentle.
All girls_____

All Americans are violent.
All Americans _____

All boys are rough.
All boys _____

All old people are doddery.
All old people_____

All the best chefs are men.
All the best chefs_____

All birth parents are responsible.
All birth parents _____

All wealthy people are snobs.
All wealthy people_____

All wives nag.
All wives_____

All babies are noisy.
All babies_____

All English people are bad at languages.
All English people_____

All teachers know all the answers.
All teachers_____

All young people are disrespectful.
All young people_____

Possible answers

All girls are gentle.
All girls are females under 18 years of age.

All Americans are violent.
All Americans are American citizens.

All boys are rough.
All boys are males under 18 years of age.

All old people are doddery.
All old people have lived for longer than young people.

All the best chefs are men.
All the best chefs are excellent cooks.

All birth parents are responsible.
All birth parents have had children.

All wealthy people are snobs.
All wealthy people have more money and/or assets than poor people.

All wives nag.
All wives are married.

All babies are noisy.
All babies are unique.

All English people are bad at languages.
All English people are British citizens.

All teachers know all the answers.
All teachers know some of the answers.

All young people are disrespectful.
All young people have had fewer life experiences than many old people.